Diabetic Desserts

Everyday Delights

Cookies & Bars

Cakes & Cheesecakes

Sweet Sensations

Company's Coming

For the Way You Live

For the Way You Live

Years ago people with diabetes were told not to eat foods with sugar. New research shows you can eat desserts and other foods made with sugar. Substituting a small portion of dessert for another carbohydrate food in your meal is the key to keeping your blood sugar in target range. It is the total amount of carbohydrate in your meal that affects blood sugar the most.

With this knowledge, we have included sugar in the *Diabetic Desserts* cookbook.

The recipes with added sugar are noted with this symbol:

The recipes with no added sugar are noted with this symbol:

Sugar Substitutes

Amount of Sugar Substitute Packets to Substitute for Granulated Sugar

Granulated Sugar	Aspartame (used in Equal®)	Sucralose (used in Splenda®)	Saccharin (used in Sweet'N Low®)
2 teaspoons	1 packet	2 teaspoons	1/5 teaspoon
1 tablespoon	1½ packets	1 tablespoon	1/3 teaspoon
¼ cup	6 packets	6 packets	3 packets
1/3 cup	8 packets	8 packets	4 packets
½ cup	12 packets	12 packets	6 packets

Facts about the Recipes

All the recipes in this book are based on the principles of sound nutrition making them perfect for the entire family. These recipes are not to be used as a substitute for medically approved meal plans.

The Dietary Exchanges are based on the Exchange Lists for Meal Planning developed by the American Diabetes Association and The American Diatetic Association. Every effort has been made to check the accuracy of these numbers. However, because numerous variables account for a wide range of values in certain foods, all analyses that appear in the book should be considered approximate.

- **The analysis of each recipe includes all the ingredients that are listed in that recipe, except for ingredients labeled as "optional" or "for garnish." Nutritional analysis is provided for the primary recipe only, not for the recipe variations.**
- **If a range is offered for an ingredient, the first amount given was used to calculate the nutritional information.**
- **If an ingredient is presented with an option ("3 tablespoons margarine or butter," for example), the *first* item listed was used to calculate the nutritional information.**

Everyday Delights

New Age Candy Apple

1 Granny Smith apple, peeled
¼ teaspoon sugar-free cherry-flavored gelatin
2 tablespoons diet cherry cola
2 tablespoons thawed frozen reduced-fat whipped topping

1. Slice apple crosswise into ¼-inch-thick rings; remove seeds. Stack apple rings in small microwavable bowl; sprinkle with gelatin. Pour cola over rings.

2. Cover loosely with waxed paper. Microwave on HIGH 2 minutes or until liquid is boiling. Let stand, covered, 5 minutes. Arrange rings on dessert plate. Serve warm with whipped topping. *Makes 1 serving*

Note: This recipe can be doubled or tripled easily. To cook 2 apples at a time, increase cooking time to 3½ minutes. To cook 3 apples at a time, increase cooking time to 5 minutes.

Nutrients per Serving

Calories	**102**	**Carbohydrate**	**23g**
Calories from Fat	**17%**	**Cholesterol**	**0mg**
Total Fat	**2g**	**Sodium**	**1mg**
Saturated Fat	**1g**	**Dietary Fiber**	**4g**
Protein	**<1g**		

DIETARY EXCHANGES: 1½ Fruit

Cinnamon Dessert Tacos with Fruit Salsa

1 cup sliced fresh strawberries
1 cup cubed fresh pineapple
1 cup cubed peeled kiwi
½ teaspoon minced jalapeño pepper (optional)
4 teaspoons sugar substitute
3 tablespoons granulated sugar
1 tablespoon ground cinnamon
6 (8-inch) flour tortillas
Nonstick cooking spray

1. Stir together strawberries, pineapple, kiwi, jalapeño pepper, if desired, and sugar substitute in large bowl; set aside. Combine sugar and cinnamon in small bowl; set aside.

2. Spray 1 tortilla lightly on both sides with cooking spray. Heat in nonstick skillet over medium heat until slightly puffed and golden brown. Remove from heat; immediately dust both sides with cinnamon-sugar mixture. Shake excess cinnamon-sugar back into bowl. Repeat until all tortillas are warmed.

3. Fill tortillas with fruit mixture and fold in half. Serve immediately. *Makes 6 servings*

Nutrients per Serving

Calories	**183**	**Carbohydrate**	**36g**
Calories from Fat	**14%**	**Cholesterol**	**0mg**
Total Fat	**3g**	**Sodium**	**169mg**
Saturated Fat	**<1g**	**Dietary Fiber**	**4g**
Protein	**4g**		

DIETARY EXCHANGES: 1½ Starch, 1 Fruit, ½ Fat

Orange Smoothies

1 cup fat-free vanilla ice cream or fat-free vanilla frozen yogurt
¾ cup low-fat (1%) milk
¼ cup frozen orange juice concentrate

1. Combine ice cream, milk and orange juice concentrate in food processor or blender; process until smooth.

2. Pour mixture into 2 glasses; garnish as desired. Serve immediately.

Makes 2 servings

Nutrients per Serving

Calories	**185**	**Carbohydrate**	**38g**
Calories from Fat	**5%**	**Cholesterol**	**4mg**
Total Fat	**1g**	**Sodium**	**117mg**
Saturated Fat	**<1g**	**Dietary Fiber**	**<1g**
Protein	**8g**		

DIETARY EXCHANGES: 1½ Starch, 1 Fruit

Raspberry Smoothies

1½ cups fresh or frozen raspberries
1 cup plain fat-free yogurt
1 cup crushed ice
4 teaspoons sugar substitute
1 tablespoon honey

Place all ingredients in food processor or blender; process until smooth. Scrape down sides as needed. Serve immediately.

Makes 2 servings

Nutrients per Serving

Calories	143	Carbohydrate	28g
Calories from Fat	4%	Cholesterol	2mg
Total Fat	<1g	Sodium	88mg
Saturated Fat	<1g	Dietary Fiber	6g
Protein	8g		

DIETARY EXCHANGES: ½ Milk, 1½ Fruit

Berry-Peachy Cobbler

4 tablespoons plus 2 teaspoons sugar, divided
¾ cup plus 2 tablespoons all-purpose flour
1¼ pounds peaches, peeled and sliced *or* 1 package (16 ounces) frozen unsweetened sliced peaches, thawed and drained
2 cups fresh raspberries *or* 1 package (12 ounces) frozen unsweetened raspberries
1 teaspoon grated lemon peel
½ teaspoon baking powder
½ teaspoon baking soda
⅛ teaspoon salt
2 tablespoons cold margarine, cut into pieces
½ cup low-fat buttermilk

1. Preheat oven to 425°F. Spray 8 ramekins or 11×7-inch baking dish with nonstick cooking spray; place ramekins on jelly-roll pan.

2. Combine 2 tablespoons sugar and 2 tablespoons flour in large bowl. Add peaches, raspberries and lemon peel; toss to coat. Divide fruit among prepared ramekins. Bake about 15 minutes or until fruit is bubbly around edges.

3. Meanwhile, for topping, combine remaining ¾ cup flour, 2 tablespoons sugar, baking powder, baking soda and salt in medium bowl. Cut in margarine with pastry blender or two knives until mixture resembles coarse crumbs. Stir in buttermilk just until dry ingredients are moistened.

4. Remove ramekins from oven; top fruit with equal dollops of topping. Sprinkle with remaining 2 teaspoons sugar. Bake 18 to 20 minutes or until topping is lightly browned. Serve warm. *Makes 8 servings*

Nutrients per Serving

Calories	149	Carbohydrate	28g
Calories from Fat	20%	Cholesterol	1mg
Total Fat	3g	Sodium	195mg
Saturated Fat	1g	Dietary Fiber	3g
Protein	3g		

DIETARY EXCHANGES: 1 Starch, 1 Fruit, 1 Fat

Iced Cappuccino

1 cup fat-free vanilla frozen yogurt or fat-free vanilla ice cream
1 cup cold strong-brewed coffee
2 teaspoons sugar substitute
1 teaspoon unsweetened cocoa powder
1 teaspoon vanilla

1. Place all ingredients in food processor or blender; process until smooth. Place container in freezer; freeze 1½ to 2 hours or until top and sides of mixture are partially frozen.

2. Scrape sides of container; process until smooth and frothy. Garnish as desired. Serve immediately.

Makes 2 servings

Iced Mocha Cappuccino: Increase amount of unsweetened cocoa powder to 1 tablespoon. Proceed as directed above.

Nutrients per Serving

Calories	**105**	**Carbohydrate**	**21g**
Calories from Fat	**0%**	**Cholesterol**	**<1mg**
Total Fat	**<1g**	**Sodium**	**72mg**
Saturated Fat	**<1g**	**Dietary Fiber**	**0g**
Protein	**5g**		

DIETARY EXCHANGES: 1½ Starch

To add an extra flavor boost to this refreshing drink, add orange peel, lemon peel or a dash of ground cinnamon to your coffee grounds before brewing.

Cookies & Bars

Cream Cheese Brownie Royale

1 package (about 15 ounces) brownie mix for 8-inch square pan
⅔ cup cold coffee or water
1 package (8 ounces) reduced-fat cream cheese, softened
1 egg
5 teaspoons sugar substitute
1 tablespoon fat-free (skim) milk
½ teaspoon vanilla

1. Preheat oven to 350°F. Coat 13×9-inch nonstick baking pan with nonstick cooking spray; set aside.

2. Combine brownie mix and coffee in large bowl; stir until blended. Pour brownie mixture into prepared pan.

3. Beat cream cheese, egg, sugar substitute, milk and vanilla in medium bowl with electric mixer at medium speed until smooth. Spoon cream cheese mixture in small dollops over brownie mixture. Swirl cream cheese mixture into brownie mixture with tip of knife.

4. Bake 30 to 35 minutes or until toothpick inserted into center comes out clean. Cool completely in pan on wire rack.

5. Cover with foil and refrigerate 8 hours or until ready to serve. Garnish as desired. *Makes 16 servings*

Nutrients per Serving

Calories	167	Carbohydrate	28 g
Calories from Fat	25%	Cholesterol	7 mg
Total Fat	5 g	Sodium	181 mg
Saturated Fat	2 g	Dietary Fiber	1 g
Protein	4 g		

DIETARY EXCHANGES: 2 Starch, ½ Fat

Carrot & Spice Bars

1 cup low-fat (1%) milk
¼ cup margarine or butter
1 cup bran flakes cereal
2 eggs
¾ cup grated carrot
⅓ cup golden raisins, coarsely chopped
1 jar (2½ ounces) puréed baby food carrots
1 teaspoon grated orange peel
1 teaspoon vanilla
2 cups all-purpose flour
¾ cup sugar
1 teaspoon baking soda
1 teaspoon ground cinnamon
¼ cup orange juice
¼ cup toasted pecans, chopped

1. Preheat oven to 350°F. Lightly coat 13×9-inch baking pan with nonstick cooking spray; set aside.

2. Combine milk and margarine in large microwavable bowl. Microwave on HIGH 1 minute or until margarine is melted; add cereal. Let stand 5 minutes. Add eggs; whisk to blend. Add grated carrot, raisins, puréed carrots, orange peel and vanilla.

3. Combine flour, sugar, baking soda and cinnamon in medium bowl. Add to carrot mixture, stirring until thoroughly blended. Spread into prepared pan.

4. Bake 25 minutes or until toothpick inserted into center comes out clean. Insert tines of fork into cake at 1-inch intervals. Spoon orange juice over cake. Sprinkle with pecans; press into cake. *Makes 40 servings*

Nutrients per Serving

Calories	**114**	**Carbohydrate**	**19g**
Calories from Fat	**26%**	**Cholesterol**	**18mg**
Total Fat	**3g**	**Sodium**	**100mg**
Saturated Fat	**1g**	**Dietary Fiber**	**1g**
Protein	**2g**		

DIETARY EXCHANGES: 1 Starch, ½ Fruit, ½ Fat

Oatmeal-Date Cookies

ADDED SUGAR

½ cup packed light brown sugar
¼ cup margarine, softened
1 egg plus 1 egg white, lightly beaten
1 tablespoon thawed frozen apple juice concentrate
1 teaspoon vanilla
1½ cups all-purpose flour
2 teaspoons baking soda
¼ teaspoon salt
1½ cups uncooked quick oats
½ cup chopped dates or raisins

1. Preheat oven to 350°F. Lightly coat cookie sheets with nonstick cooking spray; set aside.

2. Beat sugar and margarine in large bowl. Add egg, egg white, apple juice concentrate and vanilla; mix well.

3. Add flour, baking soda and salt; mix well. Stir in oats and dates. Drop dough by rounded teaspoonfuls onto prepared cookie sheets.

4. Bake 8 to 10 minutes or until edges are very lightly browned. (Centers should still be soft.) Cool 1 minute on cookie sheets. Remove to wire racks; cool completely.

Makes 36 servings

Nutrients per Serving

Calories	65
Calories from Fat	27%
Total Fat	2g
Saturated Fat	<1g
Protein	1g
Carbohydrate	11g
Cholesterol	6mg
Sodium	106mg
Dietary Fiber	1g

DIETARY EXCHANGES: 1 Starch

Lemon-Cranberry Bars

½ cup sugar substitute
½ cup thawed frozen lemonade concentrate
¼ cup margarine, softened
1 egg
1½ cups all-purpose flour
2 teaspoons grated lemon peel
½ teaspoon baking soda
½ teaspoon salt
½ cup dried cranberries

1. Preheat oven to 375°F. Lightly coat 8-inch square baking pan with nonstick cooking spray; set aside.

2. Combine sugar substitute, lemonade concentrate, margarine and egg in medium bowl; mix well. Add flour, lemon peel, baking soda and salt; stir well. Stir in cranberries; pour into prepared pan.

3. Bake 20 minutes or until light brown. Cool completely in pan on wire rack. Cut into 16 squares.

Makes 16 servings

Nutrients per Serving

Calories	104	**Carbohydrate**	15g
Calories from Fat	28%	**Cholesterol**	13mg
Total Fat	3g	**Sodium**	150mg
Saturated Fat	1g	**Dietary Fiber**	<1g
Protein	3g		

DIETARY EXCHANGES: 1 Starch, ½ Fat

Pumpkin Chocolate Chip Cookies

2 cups all-purpose flour
1 teaspoon baking soda
1 teaspoon ground cinnamon
½ teaspoon salt
¼ teaspoon ground nutmeg
¼ teaspoon ground cloves
½ cup granulated sugar
½ cup packed brown sugar
½ cup solid-pack pumpkin
¼ cup caramel-flavored low-fat yogurt
1 egg
½ cup mini semisweet chocolate chips

1. Preheat oven to 350°F. Lightly coat cookie sheets with nonstick cooking spray; set aside.

2. Combine flour, baking soda, cinnamon, salt, nutmeg and cloves in medium bowl; set aside.

3. Combine sugars, pumpkin, yogurt and egg in large bowl. Blend in flour mixture. Stir in chocolate chips.

4. Drop dough by rounded teaspoonfuls onto prepared cookie sheets. Bake 10 minutes or until firm. Remove to wire racks to cool completely. *Makes 36 servings*

Nutrients per Serving

Calories	63	**Carbohydrate**	13g
Calories from Fat	14%	**Cholesterol**	6mg
Total Fat	1g	**Sodium**	72mg
Saturated Fat	<1g	**Dietary Fiber**	<1g
Protein	1g		

DIETARY EXCHANGES: 1 Starch

Confetti Cookies

2⅓ cups all purpose flour
1½ teaspoons baking soda
¼ teaspoon salt
¼ cup margarine or butter, softened
3 ounces reduced-fat cream cheese
¾ cup sugar
¼ cup cholesterol-free egg substitute
½ teaspoon almond extract
1 cup dried fruit bits
Sliced almonds (optional)

1. Combine flour, baking soda and salt in medium bowl; set aside. Beat margarine and cream cheese in large bowl with electric mixer at medium speed until blended. Add sugar, egg substitute and almond extract; beat until well blended. Stir in flour mixture; add fruit bits.

2. Shape dough into 2 logs, each about 9 inches long. Wrap each log in waxed paper or plastic wrap. Refrigerate 1 hour or overnight.

3. Preheat oven to 350°F. Lightly coat cookie sheets with nonstick cooking spray. Cut logs into ½-inch-thick slices. Place on prepared cookie sheet. Arrange 3 almond slices on top of each cookie in decorative pattern, if desired. Bake 10 minutes or until firm to touch. Remove to wire racks to cool completely. *Makes 36 servings*

Nutrients per Serving

Calories	**74**	**Carbohydrate**	**13g**
Calories from Fat	**24%**	**Cholesterol**	**1mg**
Total Fat	**2g**	**Sodium**	**98mg**
Saturated Fat	**1g**	**Dietary Fiber**	**1g**
Protein	**1g**		

DIETARY EXCHANGES: 1 Starch

Cakes & Cheesecakes

Zucchini Spice Bundt Cake

1 package (about 18 ounces) spice or carrot cake mix
1 cup water
3/4 cup cholesterol-free egg substitute
2 tablespoons canola oil
1 medium zucchini, shredded
3 tablespoons chopped walnuts, toasted*
3/4 teaspoon vanilla
1/4 cup powdered sugar
1 to 2 teaspoons fat-free (skim) milk

To toast walnuts, spread in single layer on baking sheet. Bake in preheated 350°F oven 6 to 8 minutes or until golden brown, stirring frequently.

1. Preheat oven to 325°F. Spray 12-cup bundt pan with nonstick cooking spray.

2. Combine cake mix, water, egg substitute and oil in large bowl; mix according to package directions. Stir in zucchini, walnuts and vanilla. Pour into prepared pan. Bake 40 to 45 minutes or until toothpick inserted near center comes out almost clean. Cool 10 minutes in pan on wire rack. Invert onto wire rack; cool completely.

3. Blend powdered sugar and milk in small bowl until smooth. Drizzle glaze over cake. *Makes 18 servings*

Nutrients per Serving

Calories	**154**	**Carbohydrate**	**25g**
Calories from Fat	**28%**	**Cholesterol**	**0mg**
Total Fat	**5g**	**Sodium**	**205mg**
Saturated Fat	**1g**	**Dietary Fiber**	**<1g**
Protein	**2g**		

DIETARY EXCHANGES: 1½ Starch, 1 Fat

Chocolate Bundt Cake with White Chocolate Glaze

CAKE

1 package (about 18 ounces) chocolate cake mix
¾ cup cholesterol-free egg substitute *or* 3 eggs
3 jars (2½ ounces each) puréed baby food prunes
¾ cup warm water
2 to 3 teaspoons instant coffee granules
2 tablespoons canola oil

GLAZE (optional)

½ cup white chocolate chips
1 tablespoon milk

1. Preheat oven to 350°F. Lightly grease and flour 12-cup bundt pan; set aside.

2. For cake, beat cake mix, egg substitute, prunes, water, coffee granules and oil in large bowl with electric mixer at high speed 2 minutes. Pour into prepared pan. Bake 40 minutes or until toothpick inserted near center comes out clean. Cool in pan on wire rack 10 minutes. Invert cake onto serving plate; cool completely.

3. For glaze, combine white chocolate chips and milk in small microwavable bowl. Microwave on MEDIUM 50 seconds; stir. Microwave on MEDIUM at additional 30-second intervals until chips are completely melted; stir after each 30-second interval.

4. Pour warm glaze over cooled cake. Let stand about 30 minutes before serving. *Makes 16 servings*

Nutrients per Serving

Calories	**177**	**Carbohydrate**	**27g**
Calories from Fat	**36%**	**Cholesterol**	**<1mg**
Total Fat	**7g**	**Sodium**	**292mg**
Saturated Fat	**1g**	**Dietary Fiber**	**1g**
Protein	**4g**		

DIETARY EXCHANGES: 2 Starch, 2 Fat

Berries and Cheesecake Nesters

- 2 sheets phyllo dough, thawed
- 4 ounces reduced-fat cream cheese
- ¼ cup reduced-fat sour cream
- 3 tablespoons fat-free (skim) milk
- 1 tablespoon sugar
- 3 packets sugar substitute
- ½ teaspoon vanilla
- 1 cup blueberries or raspberries

1. Preheat oven to 350°F. Spray both sides of phyllo dough with nonstick cooking spray. Working quickly, cut each sheet of dough lengthwise into 4 strips, then cut each strip crosswise into 4 pieces.

2. Spray 8 standard (2½-inch) nonstick muffin cups with cooking spray. Press 4 phyllo squares into each cup with corners overlapping; ruffle edges to create nests. Bake 4 minutes or until golden. Cool in pan on wire rack.

3. Meanwhile, beat cream cheese, sour cream, milk, sugar, sugar substitute and vanilla in medium bowl with electric mixer at medium speed until smooth.

4. Gently remove nests from pan. Spoon 2 tablespoons cream cheese mixture into each nest; top with 2 tablespoons berries.

Makes 8 servings

Nutrients per Serving

Calories	**75**	**Carbohydrate**	**9g**
Calories from Fat	**39%**	**Cholesterol**	**9mg**
Total Fat	**3g**	**Sodium**	**98mg**
Saturated Fat	**2g**	**Dietary Fiber**	**<1g**
Protein	**2g**		

DIETARY EXCHANGES: ½ Starch, 1 Fat

Chocolate Pudding Cake

CAKE

1 cup all-purpose flour
½ cup warm fat-free (skim) milk
7 tablespoons sugar substitute
⅓ cup sugar
3 tablespoons unsweetened cocoa powder
2 tablespoons canola oil
2 teaspoons baking powder
2 teaspoons vanilla
½ teaspoon salt

SAUCE

7 tablespoons sugar substitute
¼ cup sugar
3 tablespoons unsweetened cocoa powder
1¾ cups boiling water

1. Preheat oven to 350°F. Combine all cake ingredients in large bowl; mix well. Pour into ungreased 9-inch square baking pan.

2. For sauce, sprinkle 7 tablespoons sugar substitute, ¼ cup sugar and 3 tablespoons cocoa over batter in pan. Pour boiling water over top. *Do not stir.* Bake 40 minutes or until cake has risen to top of pan and sauce is bubbling underneath. Serve immediately. *Makes 9 servings*

Nutrients per Serving

Calories	**150**	**Carbohydrate**	**26g**
Calories from Fat	**18%**	**Cholesterol**	**<1mg**
Total Fat	**3g**	**Sodium**	**246mg**
Saturated Fat	**<1g**	**Dietary Fiber**	**<1g**
Protein	**4g**		

DIETARY EXCHANGES: 1½ Starch, ½ Fat

Caribbean Cake Squares

1 package (9 ounces) yellow cake mix
½ cup orange juice
2 egg whites
2 cans (8 ounces each) crushed pineapple in juice
Additional orange juice
1 tablespoon cornstarch
½ cup slivered almonds
½ cup shredded coconut
2 large ripe bananas
1 can (15 ounces) mandarin orange segments in light syrup, drained

1. Preheat oven to 350°F. Spray 13×9-inch nonstick baking pan with nonstick cooking spray.

2. Beat cake mix, orange juice and egg whites in medium bowl with electric mixer at medium speed 2 minutes or until well blended. Spoon batter evenly into prepared pan. Bake 11 minutes or until toothpick inserted into center comes out clean. Cool completely in pan on wire rack.

3. Drain pineapple into 2-cup measure; add additional orange juice to measure 1½ cups liquid. Stir in cornstarch until smooth. Bring juice mixture to a boil in medium saucepan over high heat, stirring constantly. Boil 1 minute, stirring constantly. Remove from heat.

4. Place almonds and coconut in large skillet; heat over medium heat until lightly browned, stirring frequently.

5. Spread pineapple evenly over cake. Slice bananas; arrange over pineapple. Top with mandarin orange segments. Carefully drizzle juice mixture evenly over topping. Sprinkle with almond mixture. Cover and refrigerate 1 to 4 hours.

Makes 16 servings

Nutrients per Serving

Calories	**148**	**Carbohydrate**	**25g**
Calories from Fat	**29%**	**Cholesterol**	**<1mg**
Total Fat	**5g**	**Sodium**	**115mg**
Saturated Fat	**1g**	**Dietary Fiber**	**2g**
Protein	**2g**		

DIETARY EXCHANGES: 1½ Starch, 1 Fat

Lemon Poppy Seed Bundt Cake

- **1 cup granulated sugar**
- **½ cup (1 stick) margarine, softened**
- **1 egg**
- **2 egg whites**
- **¾ cup low-fat (1%) milk**
- **2 teaspoons vanilla**
- **2 cups all-purpose flour**
- **2 tablespoons poppy seeds**
- **1 tablespoon grated lemon peel**
- **2 teaspoons baking powder**
- **¼ teaspoon salt**
- **1½ tablespoons powdered sugar**

1. Preheat oven to 350°F. Grease and flour 10-inch bundt pan; set aside.

2. Beat granulated sugar, margarine, egg and egg whites in large bowl with electric mixer at medium speed until well blended. Add milk and vanilla; mix well. Add flour, poppy seeds, lemon peel, baking powder and salt; beat about 2 minutes or until smooth.

3. Pour into prepared pan. Bake 30 minutes or until toothpick inserted near center comes out clean; cool 10 minutes. Invert onto wire rack; cool completely. Sprinkle with powdered sugar. *Makes 16 servings*

Nutrients per Serving

Calories	**178**	**Carbohydrate**	**26g**
Calories from Fat	**34%**	**Cholesterol**	**14mg**
Total Fat	**7g**	**Sodium**	**181mg**
Saturated Fat	**1g**	**Dietary Fiber**	**1g**
Protein	**3g**		

DIETARY EXCHANGES: 1½ Starch, 1½ Fat

Enlightened Banana Upside-Down Cake

½ cup sugar
1 tablespoon water
2 tablespoons butter
2 small bananas, cut into ¼-inch slices
1½ cups all-purpose flour
2 teaspoons baking powder
½ teaspoon salt
¾ cup sucralose-based sugar substitute
¼ cup canola oil
¼ cup unsweetened applesauce
3 egg whites
1 egg yolk
½ cup low-fat buttermilk
1 teaspoon vanilla

1. Preheat oven to 325°F.

2. Combine sugar and water in small saucepan. Heat over medium-high heat, stirring mixture and swirling pan, until mixture is amber in color. Stir in butter. Immediately pour into 8-inch square nonstick baking pan. Arrange banana slices in sugar mixture.

3. Sift flour, baking powder and salt into medium bowl. Beat sugar substitute, oil and applesauce in large bowl with electric mixer at medium speed 1 minute. Beat in egg whites and yolk, 1 at a time, until blended. Beat in buttermilk and vanilla. Gradually add flour mixture; beat 1 minute or until blended.

4. Pour batter over bananas in pan. Bake 30 to 35 minutes or until toothpick inserted into center comes out clean. Cool 5 minutes in pan on wire rack; invert onto serving plate. Cool slightly before cutting into 12 pieces. Serve warm or at room temperature. *Makes 12 servings*

Nutrients per Serving

Calories	**184**	**Carbohydrate**	**27g**
Calories from Fat	**35%**	**Cholesterol**	**23mg**
Total Fat	**7g**	**Sodium**	**191mg**
Saturated Fat	**2g**	**Dietary Fiber**	**1g**
Protein	**3g**		

DIETARY EXCHANGES: 1½ Starch, ½ Fruit, 1 Fat

Sweet Sensations

Hidden Pumpkin Pies

1½ cups solid-pack pumpkin
1 cup evaporated skimmed milk
½ cup cholesterol-free egg substitute *or* 2 eggs
¼ cup sucralose-based sugar substitute
1¼ teaspoons vanilla, divided
1 teaspoon pumpkin pie spice*
3 egg whites
¼ teaspoon cream of tartar
⅓ cup honey

Or substitute ½ teaspoon ground cinnamon, ¼ teaspoon ground ginger and ⅛ teaspoon each ground allspice and ground nutmeg for 1 teaspoon pumpkin pie spice.

1. Preheat oven to 350°F.

2. Combine pumpkin, evaporated milk, egg substitute, sugar substitute, 1 teaspoon vanilla and pumpkin pie spice in large bowl; mix well. Pour into 6 (6-ounce) custard cups. Place in shallow baking dish or pan. Pour boiling water around cups to depth of 1 inch. Bake 25 minutes or until set.

3. Meanwhile, beat egg whites, cream of tartar and remaining ¼ teaspoon vanilla in medium bowl with electric mixer at high speed until soft peaks form. Gradually add honey, beating until stiff peaks form.

4. Spread egg white mixture over hot pumpkin pies. Return to oven; bake 8 to 12 minutes or until golden brown. Let stand 10 minutes. Serve warm.

Makes 6 servings

Nutrients per Serving

Calories	**148**	**Carbohydrate**	**27g**
Calories from Fat	**10%**	**Cholesterol**	**54mg**
Total Fat	**2g**	**Sodium**	**133mg**
Saturated Fat	**1g**	**Dietary Fiber**	**2g**
Protein	**8g**		

DIETARY EXCHANGES: 2 Starch, 1 Lean Meat

Creamy Strawberry-Banana Tart

1 package (16 ounces) frozen unsweetened whole strawberries, thawed
2 tablespoons plus 1½ teaspoons thawed frozen orange juice concentrate, divided
¼ cup sugar
1 envelope unflavored gelatin
3 egg whites, beaten
1 package (3 ounces) soft ladyfingers, split
4 teaspoons water
½ (8-ounce) container thawed frozen reduced-fat whipped topping,
1 medium banana, quartered lengthwise and sliced
1 teaspoon multi-colored sprinkles (optional)

1. Place strawberries and 2 tablespoons orange juice concentrate in blender or food processor; blend until smooth.

2. Combine sugar and gelatin in medium saucepan. Stir in strawberry mixture. Bring to a boil, stirring frequently.

3. Stir about half of hot mixture into beaten egg whites. Return mixture to saucepan. Cook, stirring constantly, over medium heat about 2 minutes or until slightly thickened. *Do not boil.* Pour into bowl; refrigerate about 2 hours or until mixture mounds when spooned, stirring occasionally.

4. Cut half of ladyfingers in half horizontally. Place around edge of 9-inch tart pan with removable bottom. Arrange remaining ladyfingers in bottom of pan, cutting to fit.

5. Blend remaining 1½ teaspoons orange juice concentrate and water. Drizzle over ladyfingers in pan.

6. Fold whipped topping and banana into strawberry mixture. Spoon into ladyfinger crust. Refrigerate at least 2 hours. Top with sprinkles. To serve, cut into wedges.

Makes 10 servings

Nutrients per Serving

Calories	113	**Carbohydrate**	20g
Calories from Fat	19%	**Cholesterol**	31mg
Total Fat	2g	**Sodium**	32mg
Saturated Fat	2g	**Dietary Fiber**	1g
Protein	3g		

DIETARY EXCHANGES: ½ **Starch, 1 Fruit,** ½ **Fat**

Apple Crisp

5 cups thinly sliced Granny Smith apples
⅓ cup apple cider
4½ tablespoons fat-free butterscotch or caramel ice cream topping, divided
3 tablespoons all-purpose flour
1 teaspoon ground cinnamon
1¼ cups low-fat granola with raisins
2 tablespoons margarine or butter, melted

1. Preheat oven to 350°F. Lightly coat 8-inch square baking pan with nonstick cooking spray.

2. Combine apples, cider, 3 tablespoons butterscotch topping, flour and cinnamon in large bowl. Place in prepared pan.

3. Combine granola, remaining 1½ tablespoons butterscotch topping and margarine. Sprinkle evenly over apple mixture.

4. Cover; bake 45 minutes. Uncover and bake an additional 20 to 25 minutes or until mixture is bubbly and apples are tender. Serve warm.

Makes 9 servings

Nutrients per Serving

Calories	**130**	**Carbohydrate**	**27g**
Calories from Fat	**21%**	**Cholesterol**	**0mg**
Total Fat	**3g**	**Sodium**	**82mg**
Saturated Fat	**<1g**	**Dietary Fiber**	**2g**
Protein	**1g**		

DIETARY EXCHANGES: 1 Starch, 1 Fruit, ½ Fat

Cozy Bread Pudding

- **2 cups French bread cubes**
- **2 cups multigrain bread cubes**
- **2 cups chopped unpeeled apples**
- **⅓ cup golden raisins**
- **1½ cups fat-free half-and-half**
- **¾ cup cholesterol-free egg substitute**
- **½ cup sugar substitute**
- **2 tablespoons butter flavoring**
- **1 teaspoon ground cinnamon**
- **1 teaspoon vanilla**
- **½ teaspoon ground nutmeg**
- **¼ teaspoon salt**

1. Preheat oven to 350°F. Lightly coat 2-quart baking dish with nonstick cooking spray.

2. Combine bread, apples and raisins in prepared dish. Whisk half-and-half, egg substitute, sugar substitute, butter flavoring, cinnamon, vanilla, nutmeg and salt in large bowl until blended. Pour over bread mixture; stir to coat. Let bread mixture stand 15 minutes, stirring occasionally.

3. Bake 45 to 50 minutes or until set in center. Serve warm.

Makes 8 servings

Nutrients per Serving

Calories	**120**	**Carbohydrate**	**24g**
Calories from Fat	**4%**	**Cholesterol**	**7mg**
Total Fat	**<1g**	**Sodium**	**251mg**
Saturated Fat	**<1g**	**Dietary Fiber**	**2g**
Protein	**5g**		

DIETARY EXCHANGES: 1½ Starch

Farmhouse Lemon Meringue Pie

1 frozen pie crust
4 eggs, at room temperature
3 tablespoons lemon juice
2 tablespoons reduced-fat margarine, melted
2 teaspoons grated lemon peel
3 drops yellow food coloring (optional)
1 cup cold water
½ cup sugar, divided
3 tablespoons cornstarch
3 packets sucralose-based sugar substitute
⅛ teaspoon salt
¼ teaspoon vanilla

1. Preheat oven 425°F. Bake pie crust according to package directions.

2. Separate eggs; discard 2 egg yolks. Mix lemon juice, margarine, lemon peel and food coloring in small bowl.

3. Combine water, 6 tablespoons sugar, cornstarch, sugar substitute and salt in medium saucepan; whisk until smooth. Heat over medium-high heat, whisking until mixture begins to boil. Reduce heat to medium. Boil 1 minute, stirring constantly; remove from heat. Stir ¼ cup sugar mixture into egg yolks; whisk until blended. Slowly whisk egg yolk mixture back into sugar mixture. Cook over medium heat 3 minutes, whisking constantly. Remove from heat; stir in lemon juice mixture until blended. Pour into baked pie crust.

4. Beat egg whites in large bowl with electric mixer at high speed until soft peaks form. Gradually beat in remaining 2 tablespoons sugar and vanilla; beat until stiff peaks form. Spread meringue over pie filling with rubber spatula, making sure it completely covers filling and touches edge of pie crust. Bake 5 to 10 minutes or until lightly browned. Cool completely on wire rack. Refrigerate 8 hours or overnight.

Makes 8 servings

Nutrients per Serving

Calories	170	**Carbohydrate**	25 g
Calories from Fat	42%	**Cholesterol**	54 mg
Total Fat	8 g	**Sodium**	166 mg
Saturated Fat	2 g	**Dietary Fiber**	<1 g
Protein	4 g		

DIETARY EXCHANGES: 2 Starch, 2 Fat

Strawberry Banana Cream Trifle

1 pound strawberries, sliced
½ cup sugar substitute
1 package (4-serving size) sugar-free strawberry-flavored gelatin
1 cup boiling water
1 cup ice cold water
1 package (4-serving size) banana cream fat-free sugar-free pudding and pie filling mix
1¾ cups fat-free (skim) milk
1 (10½-ounce) angel food cake, cut horizontally into thirds

1. Gently toss strawberries and sugar substitute in medium bowl; set aside.

2. Stir gelatin into boiling water in small bowl; stir 2 minutes until completely dissolved. Stir in cold water until well blended. Freeze 5 minutes to soft-set gelatin.

3. Beat pudding mix and milk in medium bowl with electric mixer at medium speed 2 minutes. Refrigerate 5 minutes to soft-set.

4. Place 1 angel food cake layer in bottom of trifle bowl. Tear another cake layer into pieces to fill in any gaps and round hole in center of cake.

5. Stir gelatin into pudding until well blended. Gently stir in strawberries. Spoon half of strawberry mixture over cake in trifle bowl. Arrange remaining cake layer on top of strawberry mixture. Fill in any gaps with remaining torn pieces of cake.

6. Top with remaining strawberry mixture. Cover and refrigerate 2 hours or until completely set. Serve chilled.

Makes 20 servings

Nutrients per Serving

Calories	59	**Carbohydrate**	13g
Calories from Fat	0%	**Cholesterol**	0mg
Total Fat	0g	**Sodium**	186mg
Saturated Fat	0g	**Dietary Fiber**	<1g
Protein	2g		

DIETARY EXCHANGES: 1 Starch

Mocha Cappuccino Ice Cream Pie

¼ cup cold water
8 teaspoons sugar substitute
1 tablespoon instant coffee granules
½ teaspoon vanilla
4 cups fat-free no-sugar-added fudge marble ice cream, slightly softened
1 vanilla wafer pie crust

1. Combine water, sugar substitute, coffee granules and vanilla in small bowl; stir until granules dissolve. Set aside.

2. Combine ice cream and coffee mixture in large bowl; stir gently until liquid is blended into ice cream. Spoon into pie crust; smooth top with rubber spatula.

3. Cover with plastic wrap; freeze about 4 hours or until firm.
Makes 8 servings

Variation: Omit pie crust and serve in dessert cups with biscotti.

Nutrients per Serving

Calories	201	**Carbohydrate**	29g
Calories from Fat	34%	**Cholesterol**	9mg
Total Fat	8g	**Sodium**	159mg
Saturated Fat	2g	**Dietary Fiber**	0g
Protein	5g		

DIETARY EXCHANGES: 2 Starch, 1½ Fat

Orange-Zested Cherry Turnovers

Nonstick cooking spray
1 can (20 ounces) no-sugar-added cherry pie filling
1 ripe medium pear or apple, peeled and diced
1 teaspoon grated orange peel
1 teaspoon vanilla
8 sheets phyllo dough, thawed
2 teaspoons powdered sugar

1. Preheat oven to 400°F. Coat large baking sheet with nonstick cooking spray.

2. Combine pie filling, pear, orange peel and vanilla in medium bowl.

3. Stack phyllo on work surface; cover with damp towel. Remove 1 phyllo sheet; keep remaining phyllo covered. Spray phyllo with nonstick cooking spray. Fold in half crosswise; spray again. Spoon rounded ⅓ cup cherry mixture onto one end of phyllo rectangle. Fold other end of phyllo over filling; seal edges together. Turn over and roll into 4×3-inch rectangle. Place on prepared baking sheet. Repeat with remaining phyllo and filling.

4. Spray turnovers with nonstick cooking spray. Bake 20 minutes. Cool 15 minutes on wire rack. Sprinkle with powdered sugar; serve immediately. *Makes 8 servings*

Nutrients per Serving

Calories	**106**	**Carbohydrate**	**21g**
Calories from Fat	**11%**	**Cholesterol**	**0mg**
Total Fat	**1g**	**Sodium**	**101mg**
Saturated Fat	**<1g**	**Dietary Fiber**	**2g**
Protein	**2g**		

DIETARY EXCHANGES: 1 Starch, ½ Fruit

Spun Sugar Berries with Yogurt Crème

2 cups fresh raspberries*
1 container (8 ounces) lemon fat-free sugar-free yogurt
1 cup thawed frozen fat-free whipped topping
3 tablespoons sugar

You may substitute any fresh berries for the fresh raspberries.

1. Arrange berries in 4 glass dessert dishes.

2. Combine yogurt and whipped topping in medium bowl. (If not using immediately, cover and refrigerate.) Top berries with yogurt mixture.

3. To prepare spun sugar, pour sugar into heavy medium saucepan. Cook over medium-high heat until sugar melts, shaking pan occasionally. *Do not stir.* As sugar begins to melt, reduce heat to low and cook 10 minutes or until sugar has completely melted and turned light golden brown.

4. Remove from heat; let stand 1 minute. Coat fork with sugar mixture. Drizzle sugar over each serving with circular or back and forth motion. Ropes of spun sugar will harden quickly. Serve immediately. *Makes 4 servings*

Nutrients per Serving

Calories	214	Carbohydrate	29g
Calories from Fat	29%	Cholesterol	16mg
Total Fat	7g	Sodium	387mg
Saturated Fat	4g	Dietary Fiber	1g
Protein	9g		

DIETARY EXCHANGES: 1 Fruit, 1 Milk, 1½ Fat

Cranberry Phyllo Cheesecakes

1 cup fresh or frozen cranberries
¼ cup plus 1 tablespoon sugar, divided
1 teaspoon grated orange peel
2 tablespoons orange juice
¼ teaspoon ground allspice
6 sheets phyllo dough, thawed
Butter-flavored cooking spray
1 package (8 ounces) reduced-fat whipped cream cheese
8 ounces vanilla fat-free yogurt
1 teaspoon vanilla

1. Preheat oven to 350°F. Combine cranberries, ¼ cup sugar, orange peel, orange juice and allspice in small saucepan. Cook and stir over medium heat until cranberries pop and mixture thickens. Set aside to cool completely.

2. Lightly coat 12 standard (2½-inch) muffin cups with cooking spray. Cut phyllo sheets in half lengthwise, then crosswise into thirds. Spray 1 phyllo square lightly with cooking spray. Top with second square, slightly offsetting corners; spray lightly. Top with third square. Place stack of phyllo squares into one prepared muffin cup, pressing into bottom and up side of cup. Repeat with remaining phyllo squares. Bake 3 to 4 minutes or until golden. Cool completely in pan on wire rack.

3. Beat cream cheese, yogurt, remaining 1 tablespoon sugar and vanilla in medium bowl with electric mixer until smooth. Spoon about ⅓ cup cream cheese mixture into each phyllo cup. Top evenly with cranberry mixture.

Makes 12 servings

Nutrients per Serving

Calories	**104**	**Carbohydrate**	**14g**
Calories from Fat	**34%**	**Cholesterol**	**11mg**
Total Fat	**4g**	**Sodium**	**113mg**
Saturated Fat	**2g**	**Dietary Fiber**	**5g**
Protein	**3g**		

DIETARY EXCHANGES: 1 Starch, ½ Fat

Phyllo dough is available frozen in most large supermarkets. To thaw dough, place the box in the refrigerator overnight. Once opened, the dough will dry out quickly. While working with phyllo, keep the unused sheets covered with plastic wrap and a damp towel. Do not lay the damp towel directly on the dough.

Raspberry Napoleons

1¼ cups low-fat (1%) milk
1 package (4-serving size) vanilla or French vanilla fat-free sugar-free instant pudding and pie filling mix
¼ teaspoon almond extract *or* 1 tablespoon amaretto liqueur
6 sheets phyllo dough, thawed
Nonstick cooking spray
2 cups fresh raspberries
2 teaspoons powdered sugar

1. Preheat oven to 350°F. Whisk milk and pudding mix in medium bowl 2 minutes. Stir in almond extract; cover and refrigerate.

2. Working quickly, place 1 phyllo sheet on work surface; spray lightly with cooking spray. Top with 2 more phyllo sheets, spraying each with cooking spray. Cut stack crosswise into 6 strips. Cut each strip in half to form 12 rectangles. Transfer rectangles to ungreased baking sheet. Repeat process with remaining 3 phyllo sheets; place on second baking sheet. Bake 6 to 8 minutes or until golden brown and crisp. Remove to wire racks to cool completely.

3. To assemble, spread half of pudding over 8 rectangles; top with half of raspberries. Repeat layers with 8 phyllo rectangles, remaining pudding and raspberries; top with remaining 8 phyllo rectangles. Sprinkle with powdered sugar before serving.

Makes 8 servings

Nutrients per Serving

Calories	130	Carbohydrate	25g
Calories from Fat	12%	Cholesterol	3mg
Total Fat	2g	Sodium	253mg
Saturated Fat	1g	Dietary Fiber	2g
Protein	3g		

DIETARY EXCHANGES: 1 Starch, ½ Fruit, ½ Fat

Cider-Poached Apples with Cinnamon Yogurt

2 cups apple cider or apple juice
1 cinnamon stick *or* ½ teaspoon ground cinnamon
2 Golden Delicious apples, peeled, halved and cored
½ cup vanilla fat-free sugar-free yogurt
½ teaspoon ground cinnamon
½ cup chopped pecans, toasted

1. Bring apple cider and cinnamon stick to a boil in medium saucepan over high heat. Boil, uncovered, 25 minutes or until liquid is reduced to about 1 cup.

2. Add apples; cover and simmer 10 minutes or until apples are just tender. Gently transfer apple halves and poaching liquid to medium bowl; cover and refrigerate until cooled.

3. Combine yogurt and ground cinnamon in small bowl; reserve 2 tablespoons. Divide remaining yogurt mixture evenly among 4 dessert dishes. Drain apple halves and place on top of sauce. Sprinkle with toasted pecans; drizzle with reserved yogurt mixture. *Makes 4 servings*

Nutrients per Serving

Calories	159	**Carbohydrate**	30g
Calories from Fat	27%	**Cholesterol**	0mg
Total Fat	5g	**Sodium**	21mg
Saturated Fat	<1g	**Dietary Fiber**	2g
Protein	2g		

DIETARY EXCHANGES: 2 Fruit, 1 Fat

Apricot and Toasted Almond Phyllo Cups

Butter-flavored cooking spray
½ cup low-fat (1%) cottage cheese
4 ounces reduced-fat cream cheese
4 teaspoons sugar substitute
1 tablespoon fat-free (skim) milk
¼ teaspoon vanilla
4 sheets phyllo dough, thawed
3 tablespoons apricot or blackberry preserves
¼ cup sliced almonds, toasted

1. Preheat oven 350°F. Spray 8 standard (2½-inch) muffin cups with cooking spray; set aside.

2. Beat cottage cheese, cream cheese, sugar substitute, milk and vanilla in large bowl with electric mixer at high speed until completely smooth; refrigerate until needed.

3. Place 1 phyllo sheet on work surface. Keep remaining sheets covered with plastic wrap and damp kitchen towel. Lightly spray phyllo sheet with cooking spray. Top with another sheet; spray with cooking spray. Repeat with remaining sheets of phyllo.

4. Cut stack of phyllo into 8 pieces using sharp knife or kitchen scissors. Gently fit each stacked square into prepared muffin cup. Bake 5 minutes or until lightly browned; cool in pan on wire rack.

5. Place preserves in small microwavable bowl. Microwave on HIGH 20 seconds or until just melted. Spoon 2 tablespoons cream cheese mixture into each phyllo cup; drizzle with 1 teaspoon melted preserves. Top with 1½ teaspoons almonds. *Makes 8 servings*

Nutrients per Serving

Calories	109	Carbohydrate	12g
Calories from Fat	41%	Cholesterol	8mg
Total Fat	5g	Sodium	174mg
Saturated Fat	2g	Dietary Fiber	1g
Protein	5g		

DIETARY EXCHANGES: 1 Starch, 1 Fat

Lemon Mousse Squares

1 cup graham cracker crumbs
2 tablespoons reduced-calorie margarine, melted
2 teaspoons sugar substitute
⅓ cup cold water
1 envelope (¼ ounce) unflavored gelatin
2 eggs, well beaten
½ cup lemon juice
¼ cup sugar
2 teaspoon grated lemon peel
2 cups thawed frozen fat-free whipped topping
1 container (8 ounces) lemon fat-free sugar-free yogurt

1. Spray 9-inch square baking pan with nonstick cooking spray. Combine graham cracker crumbs, margarine and sugar substitute in prepared pan. Press onto bottom of pan; set aside.

2. Combine cold water and gelatin in small microwavable bowl; let stand 2 minutes. Microwave on HIGH 40 seconds to dissolve gelatin; set aside.

3. Combine eggs, lemon juice, sugar and lemon peel in top of double boiler. Cook, stirring constantly, over simmering water, about 4 minutes or until thickened. Remove from heat; stir in gelatin. Refrigerate 25 minutes or until mixture is cool and begins to set.

4. Gently whisk gelatin mixture, whipped topping and yogurt until well blended. Pour into prepared crust. Cover and refrigerate 1 hour or until firm. *Makes 9 servings*

Nutrients per Serving

Calories	**154**	**Carbohydrate**	**24 g**
Calories from Fat	**29%**	**Cholesterol**	**47 mg**
Total Fat	**5 g**	**Sodium**	**124 mg**
Saturated Fat	**1 g**	**Dietary Fiber**	**1 g**
Protein	**3 g**		

DIETARY EXCHANGES: 1½ Starch, 1 Fat

Strawberry Bavarian Deluxe

½ bag whole frozen unsweetened strawberries (1 mounded quart), partially thawed
¼ cup low-sugar strawberry preserves
¼ cup sucralose-based sugar substitute
¾ cup water, divided
2 tablespoons balsamic vinegar
2 envelopes unflavored gelatin
1 tablespoon honey
½ cup pasteurized liquid egg whites
1 teaspoon vanilla
½ teaspoon cream of tartar
1 pint fresh strawberries
1 cup frozen light whipped topping, thawed

1. Chill 2-quart nonstick bundt pan or other mold in freezer. Place strawberries, preserves and sugar substitute in food processor; process until smooth.

2. Combine ¼ cup water and vinegar in small saucepan. Sprinkle in gelatin; let stand about 5 minutes or until softened. Stir in remaining ½ cup water and honey. Cook and stir over medium heat until gelatin dissolves.

3. Whisk gelatin mixture into berry mixture in medium bowl. Refrigerate, covered, until mixture is soupy but not set.

4. Beat liquid egg whites, vanilla and cream of tartar in large bowl with electric mixer at high speed until soft peaks form.

5. Gently fold egg white mixture, one third at a time, into chilled gelatin mixture until mixture is uniform in color. Pour mousse into chilled pan. Cover and refrigerate at least 8 hours or overnight.

6. Run tip of knife around top of mold. Dip mold briefly into large bowl of hot water to loosen. To unmold, center serving plate over mold. Holding firmly so mold does not shift, invert plate and mold. Shake gently to release. Remove mold; refrigerate dessert 10 to 15 minutes. Cut into wedges; serve with whipped topping and fresh strawberries.

Makes 10 servings

Nutrients per Serving

Calories	**82**	**Carbohydrate**	**15g**
Calories from Fat	**14%**	**Cholesterol**	**0mg**
Total Fat	**1g**	**Sodium**	**25mg**
Saturated Fat	**<1g**	**Dietary Fiber**	**2g**
Protein	**3g**		

DIETARY EXCHANGES: 1 Fruit

Lemon Yogurt Pudding with Blueberry Sauce

2 cups plain fat-free yogurt
¼ cup plus 4 teaspoons sugar substitute, divided
Grated peel of 1 lemon
2 tablespoons lemon juice, divided
1 teaspoon vanilla
1½ cups fresh blueberries, divided
1 tablespoon granulated sugar
2 teaspoons cornstarch

1. For pudding, line strainer with cheesecloth or coffee filter and place over bowl. Spoon yogurt into lined strainer. Cover with plastic wrap and refrigerate 12 hours or overnight.

2. Discard drained liquid. Whisk together thickened yogurt, ¼ cup sugar substitute, lemon peel, 1 tablespoon lemon juice and vanilla in large bowl until smooth. Cover and refrigerate 1 hour.

3. For blueberry sauce, mash half the blueberries with fork. Combine mashed and whole blueberries, remaining 1 tablespoon lemon juice, granulated sugar and cornstarch in small saucepan; mix well. Cook over medium-high heat 4 minutes or until mixture has thickened. Remove from heat; cool 2 minutes. Stir in remaining 4 teaspoons sugar substitute.

4. Divide yogurt mixture among 4 small dessert bowls or stemmed glasses. Top with warm blueberry sauce. Serve immediately. *Makes 4 servings*

Nutrients per Serving

Calories	**124**	**Carbohydrate**	**22g**
Calories from Fat	**3%**	**Cholesterol**	**2mg**
Total Fat	**<1g**	**Sodium**	**91mg**
Saturated Fat	**<1g**	**Dietary Fiber**	**2g**
Protein	**9g**		

DIETARY EXCHANGES: 1 Fruit, 1 Milk

Draining plain fat-free yogurt through layers of cheesecloth as described in step 1 makes what is sometimes referred to as yogurt cheese. This fat-free product can be used in place of mayonnaise or cream cheese in dips and spreads. It is also used as the base of some desserts. The liquid drained from the yogurt is called "whey." It contains protein and calcium, so instead of throwing it away use it along with milk in baked goods, such as muffins, quick breads and pancakes.

Creamy Baked Custard with Maple Syrup

2½ cups fat-free half-and-half
½ cup cholesterol-free egg substitute
¼ cup sugar
2 teaspoons vanilla
Dash ground nutmeg
3 cups boiling water
2 tablespoons maple syrup

1. Preheat oven to 325°F. Lightly spray 6 custard cups or ramekins with nonstick cooking spray.

2. Combine half-and-half, egg substitute, sugar, vanilla and nutmeg in large bowl. Pour into prepared custard cups.

3. Pour boiling water into 13×9-inch baking dish. Place custard cups in dish. Bake 1 hour and 15 minutes. (Centers will not be completely set.) Remove cups from pan; cool completely on wire rack. Cover with plastic wrap; refrigerate overnight.

4. Drizzle with maple syrup before serving.

Makes 6 servings

Nutrients per Serving

Calories	**131**	**Carbohydrate**	**23g**
Calories from Fat	**1%**	**Cholesterol**	**17mg**
Total Fat	**<1g**	**Sodium**	**139mg**
Saturated Fat	**0g**	**Dietary Fiber**	**0g**
Protein	**5g**		

DIETARY EXCHANGES: 1½ Starch, ½ Lean Meat

Index

Index

Acknowledgments

The publisher would like to thank the companies listed below for the use of their recipes and photographs in this publication.

ConAgra Foods®

Dole Food Company, Inc.

General Mills, Inc.

The J.M. Smucker Company

Unilever